James Welch

The crowning gift of heaven

James Welch

The crowning gift of heaven

ISBN/EAN: 9783337271565

Printed in Europe, USA, Canada, Australia, Japan

Cover: Foto ©Suzi / pixelio.de

More available books at **www.hansebooks.com**

THE

Crowning Gift

OF

HEAVEN.

BY J. W. WELCH.

HUNTINGDON, PA.

J. R. DURBORROW & CO., BOOK AND JOB PRINTERS.

1873.

THE BIRTH OF CHRIST.

PART FIRST.

When Eden's blooming bowers
  Were closed to guilty man,
And storm-clouds darkly lowered
  Conveying Heaven's ban:

Whilst he in gloom departed,
  The mighty scheme was laid;
God's justice was asserted,
  And hell's dark torrent stayed.

Could Heaven produce a power
  To turn the sweeping tide
Which in that fatal hour
  From Justice's throne did glide,

And yet maintain the honor
  Of God's eternal word?
'Twere surely a misnomer,
  Jehovah-Jireh God.

Behold! O, man, the beauty
   Salvation's plan displays;
How holily, astutely,
   Was formed its golden maze.

Though Justice was unable,
   Rebellious man to save,
And lift the curtain sable
   From off his hopeless grave,

And gentle Mercy weeping,
   Gazed on the moving scene;
She, too, aloof is keeping,
   As angels bright convene.

Yet Love, within the person
   Of God's most holy Son,
Incurring Hell's aspersion,
   Redemption's work begun.

While Justice unrelenting,
   And Mercy weeping stood,
Love, unto man repenting,
   Poured out the cleansing flood,

God to his creatures human,
   In sweetest accents said:
"The seed of fallen woman
   Shall bruise the serpent's head."

"For My own Son hath taken
   The place of man condemned;
'Twill not My justice weaken—
   On Him My wrath I'll send;

"For He for man's transgression
    Hath promised to atone,
Before the congregation
    That circle Heaven's throne."

And in the time appointed,
    The great Jehovah saith:
"I on Mine own Anointed
    Will pour my withering wrath."

Now down the shadowed valley
    Through which time's current flows,
Our hastening vision sallies,
    Nor ceases for repose.

And when th' allotted ages
    To eternity have flown,
Foretold by all the sages,
    The promised gift is shown;

And lo! in Bethlehem's manger,
    'Mid angel praises loud,
Appears the Holy Stranger,
    The infant Son of God.

The Jewish skeptics cavil,
    And point with haughty scorn
Toward the lowly stable
    Where Christ, their King, was born.

"Is this the great Messiah,
    Judea's mighty King,
Declared by old Isaiah
    The captives home to bring?

"Oh! where's the royal sceptre
    That He in might shall sway,
And as a Prince and Captor
    The foul oppressor slay?

"And shall not God's Messiah,
    With proud, majestic mien,
And chariot of fire,
    Appear upon the scene?

"Whilst to Him He shall gather
    The rulers of the land,
The rabbis and the fathers
    Shall sit at His right hand.

"Likewise the great Redeemer
    Must be of royal blood;
His unrestrained demeanor
    Would speak Him sent of God.

"But this pretended Savior
    We will not thus accept,
Nor will we swerve or waver;
    His offers we reject."

THE BIRTH OF CHRIST.

PART SECOND.

The veil of night has fallen
  Upon the verdant plain,
The shepherd groups recalling
  From anxious care again.

In silence deep, reclining
  Upon the ground, they lie;
The silver stars are shining
  From out a cloudless sky.

So quiet, weird and tragic
  Appears the shadowed scene,
As though the hand of magic
  Upon its face had been.

And slowly, softly, falling
  Upon their yielding frames,
Came slumber's fetters, sealing
  Their powers in his chains.

But suddenly around them
  Appears a dazzling light!
Its brilliant rays astound them
  And rend the robe of night.

A band of forms Celestial
  Their sweetest anthem raise,
And fill the air terrestrial
  With the Redeemer's praise.

"To God be ever glory,
  On earth abounding peace!"
So ran the pleasing story
  That signal'd man's release.

And brought the cheering tidings
  From Heaven's radiant court,
That Christ, on earth abiding,
  Would change the sinful heart,

And win the Father's favor—
  The light from man withdrawn;
For this a potent Savior
  Was found in His own Son.

"Come! let us haste to view Him!"
  The shepherds gaily cry,
"We'll journey gladly to Him,
  With praises swelling high,

And with the angel voices
  Our humble notes we'll blend,
While Heaven and earth rejoices
  O'er Christ, the sinner's friend!"

Thus saying, quick they hasten,
  Their homage deep to pay,
To where the guide-star glistens,
  Above where Jesus lay;

Where sages rich oblations
  Pour at His sacred feet,
The world's great consolation
  With gratitude they greet;

And with intense emotion,
  Upon the babe they gaze,
Evincing their devotion
  By shouting loud his praise.

Although by some rejected
  With insolence and scorn—
Of infamy suspected,
  Because so lowly born;

Yet, to the soul enlightened
  By wisdom from on high,
It was a scene inviting
  And pleasing to the eye.

Incipient redemption
  Before their eyes they saw;
Satanic intervention
  Could not the work destroy.

To time's remotest limit
  The holy scheme extends;
No power can condemn it
  While God His sanction lends.

DISPUTING WITH THE DOCTORS.

1.

Within the Jewish temple, 'mong the rabbis sage and gray,
Behold the youthful Jesus, as with power he displays
The wisdom that elicited the wonder of their band;
The force that clothed his arguments the Jews could not with-
stand.

2.

The humble Son of Mary and the obscure Nazarene—
His father but a carpenter, with chisel, saw and plane—
Possessor of such wisdom, was to them a mystery;
Of Heaven's golden store-house he appeared to have the key.

3.

With questions deep he plies them, till discomfited they yield:
Against their vain traditions he presents a mighty shield,
Till, seeking him, returning now his parents close the scene,
And leave them still to wonder at the gifted Nazarene.

4.

Oh! well may Israel's rulers, of his power stand in awe;
The downfall of their cherished rites the doctors soon foresaw;
The Jewish dispensation, with its altars crimson-stained,

Its priesthood, loved and honored, was most clearly on the
wane.

5.

While hidden from the Israelites, because of unbelief,
Became the bold assertions of Salvation's lovely Chief,
Yet slowly and securely rose the structure of his hand,
The great highway of holiness to Canaan's fertile land.

6.

Around their vain traditions clung the homage of their hearts,
Though waiting for Messiah, who His power should impart,
But blinded by their prejudice, they failed their King to see
Presented in this Jesus, of detested Galilee.

7.

Alas! that Israel's scions, the elect and loved of God,
Should angrily reject the Gift that He in love bestowed—
Descendants of good Abraham, who, on Moriah's brow,
The type of reeking Calvary obediently did show.

9.

Oh! weep, Jerusalem's daughters; sit in ashes on the ground;
From Judah's potent altars has gone out the light profound;
But know, that in the coming of the Man of Galilee,
A Lamp is lighted that will burn throughout eternity.

AT THE TOMB OF LAZARUS.

1.

Pale death had enshrouded the household
  Of Mary and Martha with gloom,
And swept, by his heart-chilling power,
  Their brother beloved to the tomb.

2.

Bereft of the comfort afforded
  By unrestrained brotherly love,
'Neath sorrow's drear canopy cow'ring,
  They mourn like the unmated dove.

3.

"Oh! had but the Master been present
  When death found our happy abode,
His word the intruder had banished,
  And joy to His servants bestowed.

4.

E'en now, were He here in His power,
  Our brother to life should arise,
And death's racking scenes should no longer
  Greet darkly our tear-flooded eyes."

5.

Thus sorrowed the heart-broken sisters
Bemoaned death's power to crush,
And longed for the coming of Jesus,
Believing their grief He could hush.

6.

Oh ! how their fond hearts glow'd with rapture !
When they the Deliv'rer beheld,
Receiving the cheering assurance
Their gloom should be quickly dispell'd.

7.

And now to the grave of their loved one,
Half doubting, they wend their sad way;
Yet hoping, by Faith's intercession,
A triumph o'er death they shall see.

8.

Arrived at the mouth of the cavern,
The Master's full power they own,
And Faith, indicating her presence,
Rolls off from its mouth the great stone.

9.

And now comes the test of His power
To sunder the fetters of death,
And hurl from his throne the dread monster
Whose victims bestrew his dark path.

10.

But forth rings the cry of the victor,
And death, from his iron embrace,

Releases the cold, rigid tenant
Of darkness, to life's noontide rays.

11.

Behold! at the mandate of Jesus,
   Whose tones thrill each mortal of earth,
The dead wakes to power and action,
   And, bursting his shackles, comes forth!

12.

Thus, roused by the trumpet's loud echoes,
   We shall, on the last morn of time,
Arise from our graves in bright triumph,
   To dwell in a sorrowless clime!

ON MOUNT TABOR.

1.

On Tabor's lofty summit stands
   The Man whose life was given
To save a world from Satan's bands—
   THE CROWNING GIFT OF HEAVEN!

2.

His chosen followers are dismayed!
   As to their mortal vision,
In dazzling brightness are arrayed
   Forms from the world elysian.

3.

Upon Him falls the piercing light
   Of Heaven's unveiled grandeur,
Outshining, by its radiance bright,
   All scenes of earthly splendor.

4.

Here law and prophecy combine
   In mystic adoration;
Here Moses and Elias join
   To pour a rich oblation.

5.

While law to Calvary's mighty King
    Her homage great is giving,
Prophetic counsels to us bring
    The light o'er darkness driven.

6.

Oh! glorious light from Tabor's brow,
    To cheer the soul believing!
It images the joy that glows
    Where saints are crowns receiving.

7.

Well may the trembling Peter shrink
    From rays of light immortal;
He stands upon the river's brink
    That flows from Heaven's portal.

8.

A tabernacle he would build,
    Within the halo golden,
Whose beams his doubtings calmly still,
    And his faint heart embolden.

9.

And longs his heart to sojourn here,
    Where law and mercy blending,
Inspire his soul with joy and fear,
    While angels near are bending.

10.

He fain would tarry on the mount,
    With Heaven's tenants near him,

And gaze upon life's open fount—
'Twas oped from sin to clear him.

11.

Let Tabor's light our souls inflame
With joy and peace abiding,
Until we gaze upon the Lamb,
Where crystal streams are gliding.

12.

Beyond the surging waves we'll stand,
Released from earth's commotion,
With conquering palms in every hand,
And view the jasper ocean.

13.

Then let us toil and struggle on,
Until the crown be given;
Our feet, through grace, shall stand upon
The golden streets of Heaven!

And Tabor's light shall there illume
The plains that skirt the river
That flows hard by the golden throne,
Where sits the King forever.

HIS ENTRY INTO JERUSALEM.

1.

Behold! an unusual commotion
Near the city of Jewish devotion:
I'll meekly attempt a solution
    Of this wild, tumultuous scene:
'Tis Jesus who heads the procession—
The one who for Israel's transgression
Is destined to suffer oppression,
    Insult and derision extreme!

2.

Toward the city His way He is wending,
The people their voices are blending,
His right to the sceptre defending,
    As up from their midst swells the song
That gladdens the inmates of Heaven,
As to their sweet harps it is given,
O'er plains of delight it is driven
    In melody flowing along.

3.

Behold! how they fondly adore Him:
Their garments they're casting before Him,

While angels exultingly o'er Him
  Rejoice as they silently gaze
Upon the meek King of redemption,
Who, healing all dire dissentions,
Creates in the heart pure intentions,
  Subduing all sin by His grace.

4.

Unlike the dark scene in the garden,
The purchaser of our full pardon,
The honor that Heaven awards Him
  Here in His great majesty claims.
Let men pour their richest oblation
To Jesus, the Prince of Salvation,
Who, for the whole world's preservation,
  Endured the most horrible pains.

5.

Just here, at the gates of the city
Whose rulers are strangers to pity,
Of all places this is most fitting
  To honor the great Son of Man;
O'er whose deeds of infamy weeping,
He saw how in sin they were sleeping,
And soon in remorse would be reaping
  The horrors that compass the damned!

6.

For once may the Man of Deep Sorrow
Some light from His bright kingdom borrow;
For, ere the sunrise of the morrow,
  His sad heart will carry the woe
That ever His steps has attended

Since from His bright throne He descended.
And will till his labor is ended
   And He to His Father shall go.

7.

Though joy swells each bosom around Him,
And seems with a halo to crown Him,
Yet sadness has partially found Him,
   And presses His being the while;
Oh! how could the heart of a Savior,
Though sitting beneath transient favor,
E'er fail with emotion to quiver,
   Though wearing a heart-winning smile.

8.

For on His fond heart sore are pressing
The sins that deprive of God's blessing
Each one who the gnome is caressing
   And sporting upon the abyss;
Who, charmed by the song of the syren,
Salvation's light never desiring,
To worldly renown is aspiring,
   Refusing the highway of bliss.

9.

So great is the load He is bearing,
Though sweet be the smile He is wearing,
By power He's kept from despairing,
   Because of the heavy demand
That's made by the great, loving Father;
'Tis Christ's all the straying to gather,
And bring unto pardon and favor
   The wandering children of men.

10.

Then let us remember His toiling,
The schemes of the Evil One foiling,
By sin's stain His pure nature soiling,
   To bring us to Him in the skies;
And, glad that our humble thanksgiving
The Father is freely receiving,
Our hearts in the Savior believing,
   Let songs of devotion arise.

11.

While Calvary's banner floats o'er us,
We'll echo the loud-swelling chorus,
For Jesus has trodden before us
   The Valley and Shadow of Death.
And when our grand entry we're making,
When saints from the tomb are awaking,
And earth to its centre is quaking,
   He'll crown us with victory's wreath!

IN GETHSEMANE.

1.

Dark falls the night on Gethsemane's sod,
Where in deep sorrow the Holy One trod;
Agony boundless His gentle heart wrung,
As o'er His being the sin-curse was flung.

2.

Wrapt in deep slumber His followers lie,
All unaware of the conflict so nigh;
Yeilding to nature's lethargic appeal,
Sleep's mystic mazes their senses congeal.

3.

Waked by the Master, they quickly descend
Into the depths of the cavern again;
No strong appeal which He urgently makes,
Can their locked senses completely awake.

4.

Knew they the weight that oppresses His heart,
From their dim visions they quickly would part;
Knew they the terror that threatens His bliss,
'Twould their fond hearts with deep anguish oppress.

5.

Prone on the ground, see the Sufferer lie,
Heavenward turning His tear-suffused eye;
Blood-mingled moisture appears in great drops,
As He receives from His Father the cup,

6.

Filled to the brim with His withering wrath,
Bitter the dregs of destruction and death;
Yet on His Chosen the crushing weight falls,
Sin's galling burden His spotless soul thralls!

7.

See the submission pure love here displays;
No selfish motive His action betrays;
Willingly quaffing the sin-bittered bowl,
Choosing the grief of the unshriven soul!

8.

Sad was the hour when, stripped of his might,
Lonely and drear, 'neath the dews of the night.
Jesus, the Conqueror, languishing lay,
To the strong bands of dejection a prey.

9.

Gather, weak mortals of earth's lower clime,
Witness the struggle, as Evils combine,
Hurling their shafts e'en from Hell's lurid gate!
Angels and devils the issue await.

10.

Breathless suspense in high Heaven prevails,
As the dark powers redemption assail;

Over the battlements, weeping they gaze ;
Silent the harps and the voices of praise.

11.

Over His mind how the mad surges roll,
Casting a shade o'er His infinite soul ;
Horrors unnumbered before Him arise,
Dimming the light from the pitying skies.

12.

Heaven's winged messengers warmly applaud,
Hasting to comfort the wan Son of God ;
Swift they descend from their jasper-girt home,
Through the blue veil of the star-gilded dome.

13.

In their blest mission they quickly engage—
Hark! their low murmurs His suff'rings assuage :
On their soft bosoms they pillow His head,
Soothing the heart from which pleasure had fled.

14.

Oh ! ye bright heralds of mercy and love,
In accents as sweet as the voice of the dove,
Cheering the heart by the monster, Sin, torn,
Raising the fallen, dismayed and forlorn.

15.

So opportunely thy coming appears ;
Sweetly thy voices salute the dull ears ;
Comfort abundant thy presence affords
To the faint heart of the Lord of all Lords.

16.

Nature's weak powers unaided, must yield,
Had not thy pinions o'ershadowed the field,
Comforting, cheering, and pouring in joy,
Lest the dark shadow redemption destroy.

17.

When to the mansions of joy ye return,
Where fires of devotion eternally burn,
Tidings of joy thy soft voices will sing—
Vict'ry's loved notes o'er the wide plains will ring!

18.

Come! let us sit in Gethsemane's Shade,
Where, on the Pure One our crimes were all laid:
Let its sad memory woo the hard heart;
By His deep suffering its woes we avert.

19.

Long as our hearts to His passion pulsate,
And for His coming we patiently wait,
We shall partake of the soul-stirring joy
Flowing in streams and unmixed with alloy.

20.

And if we faithful remain until death,
On His blest bosom we'll yield our last breath,
And on the shores of eternity sing
Glad hallelujahs to Jesus, our King.

HIS ARREST.

1.

The night's sable folds o'er the Kedron has fallen,
  And darkness is reigning sublime o'er the scene;
Sad thoughts to the mind of the Savior appalling,
  Become more intense 'neath the torch's red gleam.

2.

Now o'er the brook file the minions of Satan,
  Their murderous presence is tainting the air;
Dark Mammon's fell poison their hearts is elating,
  And painting their sky with his blandishments fair.

3.

Ah! fatal delusion, their footsteps alluring,
  The demon prevails, leading captive the right;
By wily deception His person securing
  Within their dread power ere the dawn of the light.

4.

But, see the meek subject of all this confusion,
  As calmly He stands with His followers dear,
Aroused by their cries from His nook of seclusion,
  Demanding the reason why thus they appear:

5.

" Whom seek ye?" he cries, to their leader advancing:
" Why come ye out hither with lurid display?"
But 'neath His firm gaze the rude soldiery wincing,
Would fain the arrest of the Savior delay.

6.

How firm he appears, by the weapons surrounded !
Nor fears He the warlike aspect of the band,
For to their base hearts the alarm has sounded—
Before God's Messiah they tremblingly stand.

7.

They fall to the ground, by His presence o'erpowered:
The current of life in its course is withheld,
As, fearful and pale, 'neath His questions they cower,
Nor soon from their hearts is the terror dispelled.

8.

But yielding His hands to the thong of His captors,
The great King of Kings is the pris'ner of man,
While seraphic.beings, foregoing their rapture,
With poised pinions, weeping, the moving scene scan.

9.

How vain the attempt, had not Heaven's high order
Decreed the free gift of the Infinite Son !
Inscribed by the pen of the sacred recorder,
Through ages of darkness in triumph it runs.

10.

Oh ! gentle inhabitants of the Great City,
Whose crystalized walls rise majestic and bright—
Whose heaven-born senses, o'erflowing with pity,
Constrain you to gaze on this tragical sight,

11.

Go wing your swift way to the golden-bound portals
That opes on the realms of eternal delight;
Though sad be the tidings to ignorant mortals,
Yet happiness reigns in the regions of light.

12.

Though fainting disciples behold him arrested,
Before the procurator haughty to stand,
By men to be smitten, condemned and detested,
To Calvary led by the rabble's demand,

13.

Yet inside the veil that obscures mortal vision,
Preventing a view of the glorified plains,
Where o'er the quick senses the bright fields elysian,
Will cast a sweet haze when life's pilgrimage wanes,

14.

Around the great Throne where all happiness centres,
Is joy as the great consummation draws nigh,
For soon guilty man may the holy place enter,
And quaff the clear water of life flowing by.

15.

Oh! sheath thy fierce weapon, impetuous Peter!
The cup of God's anger the victim must take;
Yea, though to His taste the contents are most bitter,
In love He is suffering, vain man, for thy sake!

16.

'Tis not by the power of the sword that salvation
Is brought to the sons of degenerate man;
But by the Atonement is sent to all nations
The mercy that flows from the great Father's hand.

17.

And thus by the fiendish device of the creature,
   The pure Son of God to His trial is led;
Submission complete on his heavenly features
   In lucid effulgence is visibly spread.

18.

Oh! may our glad hearts, in their swelling emotion,
   Forget not the homage that to Him we owe,
Who, long before chaos crowned mountain and ocean,
   Existed where pleasures eternally flow.

19.

And when the fond ties of the creature shall sever,
   Releasing our souls from this casket of earth,
Around the Blest Master exulting we'll gather,
   And all the bright scenes of our journey rehearse.

20.

Far out o'er the glory-crowned valleys of Eden
   Shall ring glad narrations of victories gained;
How Hell's darkest forces, all dimly receding,
   Declared us the victors, through Jesus' great name.

21.

Then backward shall flow our swift thoughts to the Garden,
   Where He the bound captive of Judas became;
Where willingly He, to secure our full pardon,
   Was covered with infamy, sorrow and shame.

22.

Around His great Throne, where the clear, pearly River
   Of Life in its beauty transparently flows;
Where, on the pure air the glad music shall quiver
   From hearts that no shadow of sorrow disclose.

23.

There dwells in transfigured delight the freed spirits
Of all who have trodden the path of the just:
Redeemed from the hand of despair by His merit.
Their bodies in hope intermingle with dust.

24.

Though once the weak captive, betrayed and forsaken.
Before the tribunal of sin-laden man,
He now in His power the sceptre has taken,
Whilst angels and mortals obey His command.

HIS TRIAL.

1.

Caiphas, High Priest of the Jewish tribes,
In dignity o'er the council presides,
When Jesus, the subject of jeering and jibes.
   Before him is fiercely arraigned;
But death, at his cruel and heartless command,
Upon Him refuses to raise his red hand!
Next, in the stern presence of Pilate, the band
   With Jesus, their victim, are seen.

2.

Before the tribunal they clamoring cry,
Desiring that He in the robber's stead die,
They, in their mad phrenzy, all reasoning defy—
   Let Him for the nations expire!
With vigor they urge him—"Send forth the decree :
'Let this vile deceiver be hanged on a tree!'
Then from foul blasphemy shall Israel be free,
   And wrath of Jehovah most dire."

3.

But Pilate, in mercy, refuses to lend
His aid to the evils that ignobly blend,

The tide of destruction afar to extend,
   By adding to infamy's roll
The crowning event that would hurl to the tomb
The innocent Prophet in youth's ruddy bloom,
Whose actions of mercy His pathway perfume,
   And gladden the perishing soul.

4.

He pleads the dark cause of this meek, mystic King,
With whose deeds of wonder all Judea rings,
O'er whose thorny path stern misfortune e'er flings
   Dark shades to embitter life's stream;
And moved with compassion he seeks to release
The gentle Dispenser of Pardon and Peace,
At whose mighty touch human sufferings cease,
   Dispersed by fond Heaven's bright beams.

5.

But pitiless envy goads on the rude mob,
Whose hearts, unaccustomed to sympathy's throb,
Would of life's possession the Holy One rob,
   Thus crushing by one final blow
This Jesus whose power frustrates all their schemes,
Bedimming the lustre of Israel's bright dreams,
Which through the dark past did in silvery gleams
   The hope of Messiah bestow.

6.

'Tis thus they the boon of the Father reject,
His kind offer treating with idle neglect,
And failing to render to Him the respect
   That they as His favored ones owe.
Their King and Messiah e'en now they behold,

Who, coming to gather the lost of His fold,
Is willing to lavish rich treasures untold,
   Which from mercy's fountain do flow.

7.

The promise that gilds the long vista of years,
Conveyed by the line of loved Israel's seers,
E'en now in its fulness unto them appears
   The day-star, arising in power
To shed a bright ray on the fast falling night,
Obscuring the brilliance of Judah's pale light,
And shaking the structure of crumbling might
   Which once to the heavens did tower.

8.

" What ill hath He done?" the proud Roman inquires;
" To no earthly sceptre His true heart aspires:
Oh! cease the mad cravings of malice most dire,
   And free from His fetters the Man,
Who, walking your streets as a Herald of Truth,
Assumes a demeanor so low and uncouth—
Who, e'en from the days of His earliest youth,
   No ambitious fancies did scan."

9.

But louder their fierce accusations arise,
Lest some timely friend, by a cunning device,
The Roman may from his firm purpose entice,
   And thwart their inhuman designs.
The guilt of His blood they are willing to bear,
Though deep as the chasm of utter despair,
Where Hell's lurid light on the lone victim glare—
   Who in its dark cavern may pine.

10.

" Behold Him !" the Governor feelingly cries,
" Beneath the stained hand of His brethren He dies !
To envy and hatred a free sacrifice
   He yields His last tremulous breath.
Oh! hearken, ye Jews, to humanity's call;
Permit not the veil of bleak vengeance to fall
Upon your steel'd hearts, like a funeral pall,
   Exulting in Jesus' death!"

11.

And longer unable to quell their demands,
He yields the Great Prisoner into their hands,
And, clothing His form in mock royalty's bands,
   They bend the false, suppliant knee.
His sacred head pierced by the thorn-woven crown,
Till from His fair brow the red blood trickles down,
Yet in Him no sign of resentment is found—
   He suffers by Heaven's decree.

12.

Oh! let us preserve this unequalled display
Of love by our Savior, while life's fitful ray
Continues to 'lumine these temples of clay;
   And when from life's scenes we depart,
On faith's mighty pinions our spirits shall soar
To hail Him with joy on the glorified shore,
Where we shall remain, to go out nevermore,
   And bask in ineffable day.

HIS CRUCIFIXION.

Up Calv'ry's steep and rugged side,
    A frantic concourse urge their way;
Impe'l'd by hatred's madd'ning tide,
    They, chafing, will not brook delay.

Within this phrenzied circle moves
    A haggard, yet undaunted, form;
The meekness of the plaintive dove
    Is mirrored in His features wan.

And, heeding not the din that falls
    So harshly on His sens'tive ear,
In answer to fair mercy's call—
    'Tis His the crushing cross to bear.

Thus staggering 'neath the ponderous beam,
    He labors up the wearying steep,
Whilst Heaven imparts no radiant gleam,
    Despondency at bay to keep.

Now, fainting 'neath the load He bears.
    Unable longer to sustain
The galling weight, His murderers
    Relieve the excess of His pains.

Upon a native of Cyrene
  They lay the gibbet, then in haste
Resume their journey toward the scene
  Where Pity hides her tearful face.

At length they reach the dreary spot—
  That gloom-encircled place of skulls:
'Tis here the battle must be fought,
  That from his throne the monster hurls.

And quickly now they rear the cross,
  A felon vile on either side;
Their maledictions at Him thrust,
  Nor strive their groundless hate to hide.

Around its base, with tearful mien,
  His faithful followers, filled with grief:
His friends till death they e'er have been.
  Yet lack the power to give relief.

Whilst in the background dim, convene
  A flame-scarred horde of Satan's realm;
They, jeering, would His soul serene,
  With doubt's black surges overwhelm.

Oh! how they o'er His woes exult!
  Evincing bursts of hellish joy,
The while they heap their foul insults
  Upon the King of Heaven high!

Upon a molten lava sea
  Within the regions of the damn'd,
Nude devils dance in ecstacy
  As life pours out its golden sands.

Out o'er the plains of mornless night,
  In piercing tones brief vict'ry's notes
Take now their Heaven-defying flight,
  And o'er the dismal chasm float.

And as the sinless Son of God
  In agony extreme expires,
Each cell within the dark abode
  Re-echoes with the jargon dire.

All Hell rejoices as the pall
  Of death athwart the scene is thrown,
And flashing from its gloomy walls
  A momentary power is shown.

For to the eye which fails to pierce
  The veil that dims Golgotha's scene,
No tower of redemption rears
  Its summit clothed with peace serene.

Thus Satan's unprophetic gaze,
  Unable through the mist to scan
The structure of salvation raised
  For vile, unfaithful, fallen man,

Rejoices in a short-lived bliss,
  That soon must vanish as the dew,
And power's fancied gleam erased,
  No longer gilds with hope's bright hue.

But as the moments hasten on
  Toward the fiercest of His woes,
O'er nature's face a veil is drawn
  To hide the horrors here disclosed.

The sun's keen rays refuse to pierce
    The gloom, upon the scene to gaze
Where raged the contest long and fierce,
    Waged for Apostate Adam's race.

And as the midnight shadows lie
    Upon the earth in misty gloom,
See the I Am His power display—
    The dead in Jesus leave the tomb!

The temple's veil in twain is rent,
    Declaring Jewish off'rings void:
For this is the Messiah sent
    To quench their fires with His blood.

No more shall Israel's rites appease
    The anger of the King of Kings;
They have no merit now to please,
    Or turn the point of Satan's sting.

No more the smoke of sacrifice,
    Upon the balmy evening air
Shall to the God of Jacob rise,
    And pardon to his sons declare;

For now a nobler off'ring burns
    Upon an altar greater far.
No less a ransom e'er shall turn
    His wrath, or mercy's boon secure.

For this, as spoken by the seers,
    It well became the loving Son
To bear the scoffing and the jeers
    Which were in malice at Him thrown.

Thus by His meritorious death
  He purchased every sinful soul,
And with His last expiring breath,
  Declared His conquest of the world!

And as the moving picture fades
  From Fancy's graven scenery,
What gratitude each heart pervades
  Which feels the light of Calvary!

Our sympathies shall centre there
  While life's mysterious current flows;
And when our spirits cleave the air,
  It will exquisite bliss bestow.

Then from the consecrated cross
  They'll spread their pinions on the breeze,
And join the great undying host
  Who on the Mighty Conqueror gaze.

There Calvary's power inspires each tongue,
  And fills each raptured, bounding heart;
There loudly swells redemption's song,
  Where saved and Savior ne'er shall part!

'Twas Calvary's merit stayed the tide
  That swept in mighty torrents on;
Its turbid waters now subside,
  As back its surging waves are thrown.

In Calvary's anguish culminates
  The sufferings of Eden's King,
Who, through the massive golden gates,
  Came down his lost ones home to bring.

And when from mundane scenes releas'd,
We on the great Redeemer gaze,
'Twill fill each heart with rapt'rous bliss,
To dwell with Him through countless days.

HIS RESURRECTION.

In the dark sepulchre, silent and lonely,
    Lies the stark form of the poor Nazarene;
Loved by the Gallilean fishermen only,
    And the fond Marys who haste to the scene.

Ere the soft light of the rose-tinted morning
    Falls on the hills in enchanting array,
Ushering day, on its journey returning,
    With deep emotion they hasten away.

Great scalding tears through their lashes are pressing,
    Showing their love for the Master so dear;
Cheerless their hearts 'neath the cloud so distressing,
    Whose murky shadow enhances their fear.

But a bright being the mourners discover,
    Who has removed the obstructions with haste:
And the great stone, which the entrance did cover,
    By Divine Power is hurled from its place!

Silent they gaze on this child of the valleys,
    Where bloom the flowers of perpetual spring;
There in their beauty the seraphim rally,
    Sweeping the throne on their jubilant wings.

6

"Seek ye the Master in death's mouldy cavern?"
　The lovely tenant of Paradise cries;
"Know that the Gift of Omnipotent Heaven
Must from the tomb in His majesty rise,

Scaling the walls that forbiddingly tower,
　Barring a sin-condemned world from release!
Thus He achieves, by His infinite power,
　Victr'y o'er Satan—securing man's peace.

Yes; the great Jesus indeed has arisen,
　Crushing the last of man's merciless foes:
Bursting the bands of His granite-bound prison,
　Though flaming legions their arms interpose!"

Thus speaks the angel to Mary, who's weeping
　O'er the dark vault where the Savior had lain:
He whom she deemed in death's bonds to be sleeping,
　Stolen away by some miscreant hand!

"Mary!" the voice soft and tender is falling
　On the poor sorrowing follower's ear,
Heart-cheering scenes to her memory recalling.
　Of the home-circle when Jesus was there.

Quickly she turns to behold the kind Master:
　To His blest arms she would lovingly haste:
High beats her pulses, yet faster and faster
　Deep prints of sorrow by joy are effaced.

But He eludes all her tender embraces,
　Kindly declaring His work incomplete:
Yet He has power to banish grief's traces,
　Ere He assumes His sin-conquering seat.

Softly and faintly she falters, "Rabboni!"
  Teeming with love is her wild, throbbing heart;
Fondly she gazes upon the Atoner;
  From His blest presence she ne'er would depart.

" Tell my disciples and impulsive Peter,
  That I have sundered the chains of the slave:
Though the huge conflict to me was most bitter,
  Yet I have scattered the gloom of the grave!"

Swiftly she flies to His lonely adherents,
  And the glad tidings to them she imparts;
But overawed by her frantic appearance,
  Mystic delusions seize hold on their hearts.

But, on their secret assemblage intruding,
  Soon in their presence He openly stands!
Words of encouragement sweet interluding
  With invitations to view His torn hands.

Yet feeble faith fails to comprehend fully
  All the deep scheme of redemption from sin;
Nature's dull powers conceive very slowly
  How He the prize by His rising shall win.

" Come! doubting Thomas, reach hither thy finger;
  Thrust thy rude hand in my spear-mangled side!
Let no dark shade in thy bosom now linger;
  Know that 'tis He who on Calvary died!"

Faith now declares all misgivings are banished:
  By these deep mysteries he's greatly awed;
Swift as the wind does his unbelief vanish;
  Hear him exclaiming—"My Lord and my God!"

Thus, by His presence, the gloom He has lighted.
   That in dense volumes enshrouded the grave,
Cheering the hearts of a people benighted,
   Winning the title of " Mighty to Save!"

" Soon I shall rise!" He exclaims, "to My Father:
   Where, on the mediatorial throne,
I shall the straying of all nations gather
   To the delights of a sorrowless home!"

" Take ye My blessings: remember My warnings:
   Watch and be ready; faith's helmet have on:
Thus, while My grace all thy lives is adorning,
   Ye shall prepare for eternity's dawn.

Wage ye the warfare till Satan's dark forces
   Fly from the glitter of brave christian steel,
Till his great army in panic disperses,
   And his fierce onslaughts, by love, are repelled.

Then shall ye sit mid the light that is streaming,
   Lucid and wide, o'er the glorified plains,
Where the pure joy of the Father is beaming,
   And love infinite eternally reigns.

HIS ASCENSION.

The Savior stands amid His band,
  His earthly mission all fulfilled :
He, at the Father's own command,
  Has shown obedience to His will.

The scheme of free salvation wrought,
  And all its mighty struggles past,
He now a quiet nook has sought,
  Reviewing all His conflicts vast.

He, ere He speeds His happy flight,
  To fill the Intercessor's seat,
His band incites to truth and right,
  By pointing to His vict'ry great.

Through scenes of darkness and of gloom
  He kept secure the sacred trust—
E'en through the portals of the tomb,
  The heritage of mortal dust.

And now he stands upon the line
  Where mortals taste immortal bliss,
And gazes on His work sublime,
  Which gives to man eternal peace.

And as upon His chosen few,
　Like incense sweet His blessing falls,
Their vows they solemnly renew
　To heed fair Mercy's plaintive calls.

With retrospective vision, now
　He scenes surveys of pain and woe,
When He in innocence did bow
　To dark oppression's torrent low.

He gazes on the victor's meed
　Presented to His rapturous view,
From earth's debasing influence freed,
　He cleaves the veil of ether blue;

And through the misty cloud that hides
　Elysian scenes from mortal gaze,
The conquering Christ so swiftly glides,
　Whilst men and angels shout His praise.

The heavenly host around the throne,
　With shouts of ecstacy are seen
To greet with songs the Holy One
　Who paid the penalty of sin.

And on the brow of Sorrow's Child
　They place the conq'ror's sparkling crown;
By sin's pollutions undefiled,
　He by His Father's side sits down.

He now in majesty assumes
　The power that to His name belongs,
Death's shadowed valley to illume,
　And fill each heart with vict'ry's song.

THE CROWNING GIFT OF HEAVEN.

Behold! He sits endowed with power
    To raise the faint, despondent heart,
And, from this most important hour,
    Good gifts to needy man impart.

Oh, come! ye straying souls that roam
    Through shades unblessed by mercy's ray,
Forsake the dense, depressing gloom
    That hovers o'er thy cheerless way.

Come! fall in anguish at His feet,
    Who suffered 'neath the smiter's rod:
Whose mighty conquest now complete,
    Sits pleading by the throne of God.

His arm the vengeful weapon stays,
    Which on the sinful head would fall!
Was ever love so great displayed?—
    Releasing man from Satan's thrall.

How great the Gift to mortal given,
    To open wide the healing stream!
Naught else could still the wrath of Heaven,
    Or claim the power to redeem.

For this let men their praises pour,
    In melting strains, to earth's extent,
To Him who liveth evermore—
    Whose pains the rocks in chasms rent!

Let all the world to Him award
    The honor that to God belongs;
Their voices raise with sweet accord,
    And fill the air with holy songs.

Awake! ye echoes of the throne;
   Ring forth o'er all creation's plain!
In honor of the light that shone
   From Heaven, on the head of man.

THE END.

www.ingramcontent.com/pod-product-compliance
Lightning Source LLC
Chambersburg PA
CBHW021555270326
41931CB00009B/1228